Your Bones

by Terri DeGezelle

Consultant:
Marjorie Hogan, M.D.
Associate Professor of Pediatrics, University of Minnesota
Pediatrician, Hennepin County Medical Center

Bridgestone Books
an imprint of Capstone Press
Mankato, Minnesota

Bridgestone Books are published by Capstone Press
1710 Roe Crest Drive, North Mankato, Minnesota 56003
www.capstonepub.com

Library of Congress Cataloging-in-Publication Data
DeGezelle, Terri, 1955-
    Your bones / by Terri DeGezelle.
    p. cm.—(Bridgestone science library)
    Includes bibliographical references and index.
    Summary: Introduces bones, their makeup and function, bone diseases, and how
to keep bones healthy.
    ISBN-13: 978-0-7368-1146-0 (hardcover)
    ISBN-10: 0-7368-1146-X (hardcover)
    ISBN-13: 978-0-7368-3350-9 (softcover pbk.)
    ISBN-10: 0-7368-3350-1 (softcover pbk.)
    1. Bones—Juvenile literature. [1. Bones.] I. Title. II. Series.
QP88.2 .D44 2002
612.7'5—dc21

        2001003592

Editorial Credits
Rebecca Glaser, editor; Karen Risch, product planning editor; Linda Clavel, designer;
    Alta Schaffer, photo researcher; Nancy White, photo stylist

Photo Credits
Capstone Press/Gary Sundermeyer, 4, 10 (all), 12
David M. Phillips/Visuals Unlimited, 14
Digital Vision Ltd., cover (right)
Medical Plastics Laboratory, Inc., 1, 8
RubberBall Productions, cover (left)
Unicorn Stock Photos/Eric R. Berndt, 16; Jean Higgins, 18
W. S. Ormerod, Jr./Visuals Unlimited, 20

Printed in the United States of America in Eau Claire, Wisconsin.
052013   007417R

Table of Contents

Fun Fact

Babies are born with 300
bones. Many of their bones
join together as they grow.
Adults have 206 bones.

Your Bones

Bones are the framework of your body. Without bones you could not sit, stand, or walk. Bones allow you to bend over to pick up a ball. Bones support your body and protect your organs. All the bones in your body together are called your skeleton.

organ
a part of the body that does a job; the heart and lungs are organs.

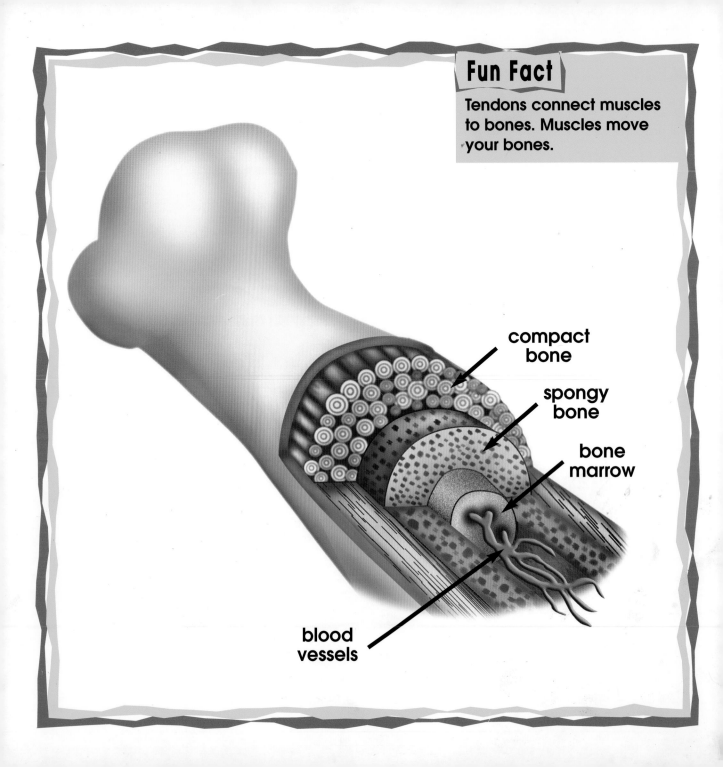

Fun Fact

Tendons connect muscles to bones. Muscles move your bones.

compact bone

spongy bone

bone marrow

blood vessels

Inside Your Bones

Your bones have three layers. Compact bone is the hard, white outer layer. The next layer is spongy bone. This layer is hard but has many holes. Bone marrow forms the center layer. Blood vessels run through the bone marrow.

blood vessel
a tube that carries blood throughout your body

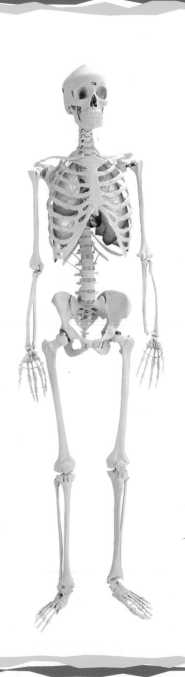

Bones Support and Protect

Bones support your body and protect your organs. Your legs and feet support your weight so that you can stand. Your spine supports your back and protects your spinal cord. Ribs protect the heart and lungs. Your skull protects your brain and eyes.

spinal cord

a thick cord of nerves that carries signals between the brain and the rest of the body

Fun Fact

Joints are named by the way they move. Elbows and knees are called hinge joints. Your shoulders and hips are ball-and-socket joints. Your neck is a pivot joint.

Joints

The place where two bones meet is a joint. Your skeleton can bend at joints. Your knees bend like a door hinge. Your shoulder joints allow your arms to rotate. The joint in your neck allows you to turn your head.

rotate

to turn around in a circular motion

Bones Store Minerals

Your body needs minerals to stay healthy. Bones store minerals such as calcium and phosphorus. Bones send the minerals into the blood when other body parts need them.

mineral

a substance found in nature that your body needs to stay healthy

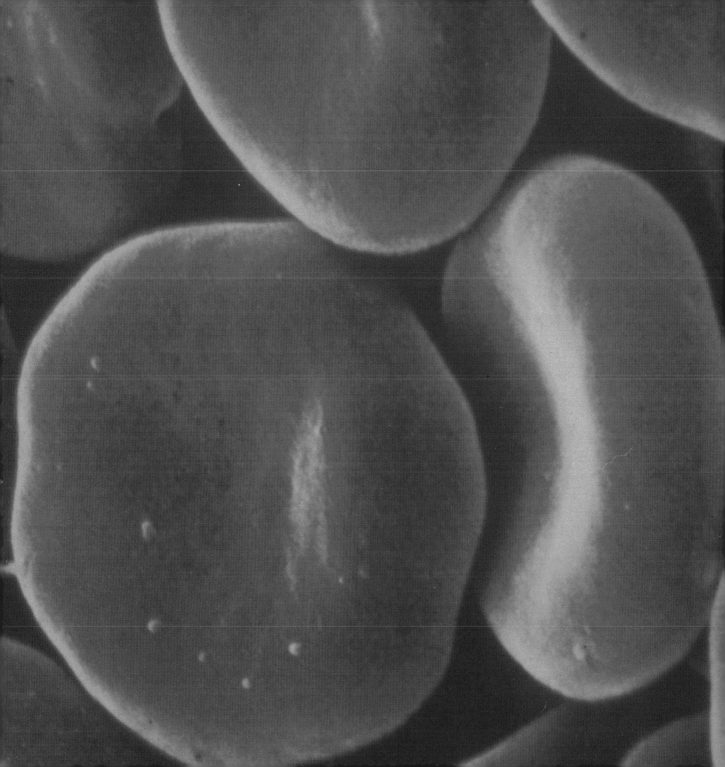

Bones Make Blood Cells

Bone marrow is a soft, sticky matter in the center of your bones. Bone marrow makes red blood cells and white blood cells. Red blood cells carry oxygen. White blood cells fight illnesses.

oxygen

a colorless gas found in air; people need to breathe oxygen to live.

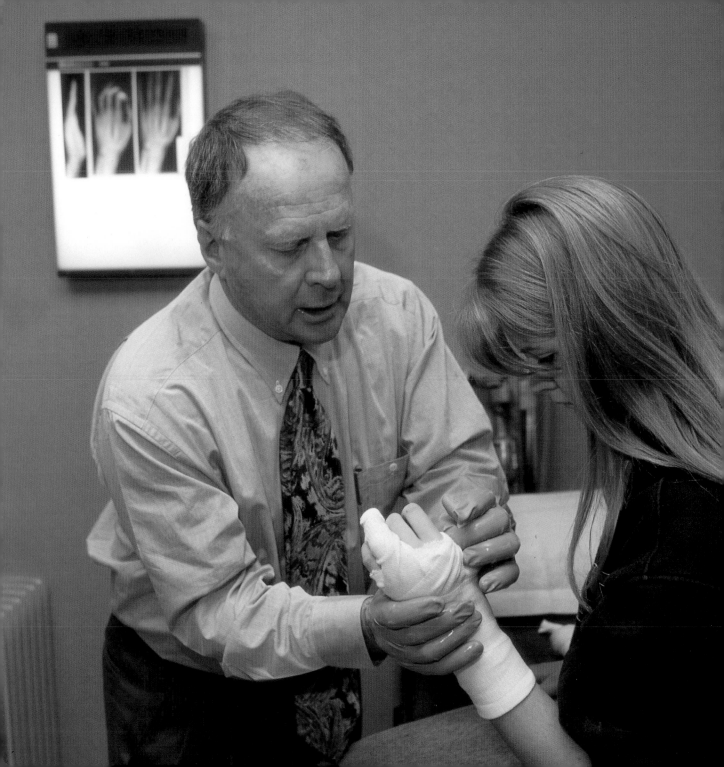

Broken Bones

A bone can break when you fall.
Doctors can set a bone so it can heal.
They use casts, pins, or screws to hold
a bone together. New bone cells grow
over a broken bone. The cells make a
patch called a callus. A healed bone is
as hard as the bone was before it broke.

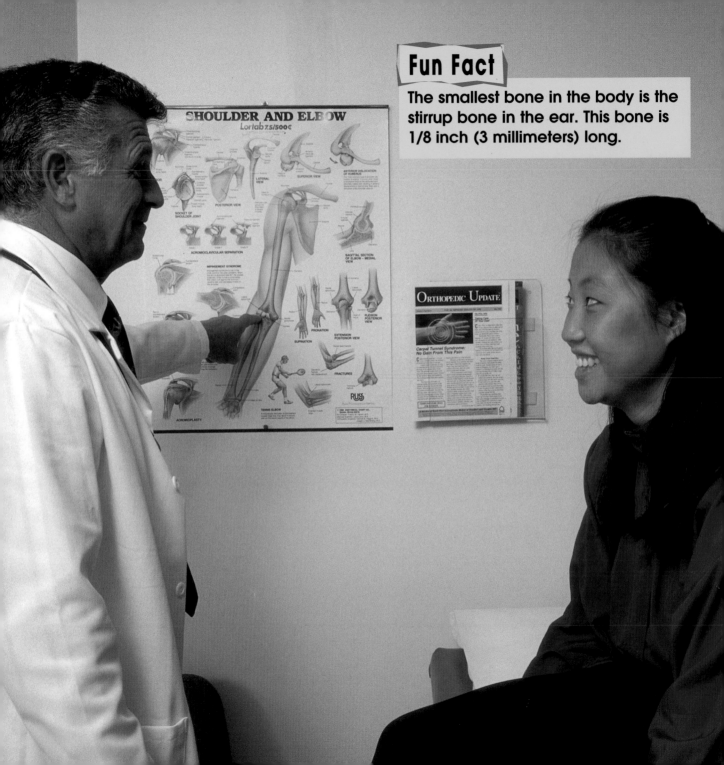

SHOULDER AND ELBOW

Fun Fact

The smallest bone in the body is the stirrup bone in the ear. This bone is 1/8 inch (3 millimeters) long.

ORTHOPEDIC UPDATE

Carpal Tunnel Syndrome:
No Gain From This Pain

Bone Diseases

Diseases can affect bones. Children can get rickets if they do not get enough vitamin D. This disease makes bones soft and weak. Scoliosis is when the spine curves sideways. Scientists do not know what causes scoliosis.

vitamin

a natural substance that you need for good health

Fun Fact

More than half of the
bones in your body are
in your hands and feet.

Healthy Bones

Bones need calcium, phosphorus, and vitamin D to stay healthy. You get calcium from milk and other dairy foods. Phosphorus is found in beef, beans, milk, and many other foods. You get vitamin D by eating fish and by being out in the sun.

Hands On: Make a Model Spine

Your spine is made up of 26 bones called vertebras. Disks make a cushion between each vertebra. You can build a model to see how the spine works.

What You Need

4 feet (120 centimeters) of yarn
26 rigatoni noodles
25 soft, round gummy candies with holes in them

What You Do

1. Tie and knot one end of the yarn to the first rigatoni noodle. The noodle is like a vertebra.
2. Thread five more noodles on the yarn.
3. Hold the yarn at the ends of the noodles and bend the string of noodles. Do the noodles move easily? Do they scrape against each other? Do they chip or crack?
4. Remove all the noodles from the string except the first one.
5. Thread a piece of candy on the yarn. The soft candy is like a disk.
6. Add a rigatoni noodle. Alternate adding a piece of candy and a noodle until you have used all the noodles and candies.
7. Tie the end of the yarn to the last rigatoni noodle.
8. Bend the string of noodles and candies. Do the soft candies help the noodles to move more easily? Do the noodles rub against each other?

The noodles are hard and strong like your vertebras. The candies are soft and cushiony like the disks of your spine. The small bones and cushions between the bones help you bend and twist.

Words to Know

bone marrow (BOHN MA-roh)—the soft jellylike material in the middle of bones where blood cells are made

calcium (KAL-see-uhm)—a soft, silver-white mineral found in teeth and bones

callus (KA-luhs)—a mass of tissue that forms around a broken bone

joint (JOINT)—a place where two bones meet; knees, elbows, and hips are joints.

organ (OR-guhn)—a part of the body that does a job; the heart and lungs are organs.

phosphorus (FOSS-fur-uhss)—a mineral the body needs to form strong bones and teeth

rickets (RIK-its)—a disease that makes children's bones become soft because of a lack of vitamin D

spinal cord (SPINE-uhl KORD)—a thick cord of nerves that carries signals between the brain and the rest of the body

Read More

Goode, Katherine. *Skeleton and Muscles.* Bodyworks. Woodbridge, Conn.: Blackbirch Press, 2000.

LeVert, Suzanne. *Bones and Muscles.* Kaleidoscope. New York: Benchmark Books/Marshall Cavendish, 2001.

Wood, Lily. *Skeletons.* Scholastic Science Readers. New York:Scholastic Reference, 2001.

Internet Sites

FactHound offers a safe, fun way to find Internet sites related to this book.

Go to *www.facthound.com*

He'll fetch the best sites for you!

Index